KATHLEEN PARTRIDGE'S
Get Well Book

To

....

From

....

Jarrold Colour Publications, Norwich.

GOD BLESS YOU

Keep these verses by your bedside
Keep these pictures in your mind
With a world of flowers and bird songs
For your waking eyes designed.

Keep the joy of all God's goodness
When the uphill pathway wends
Secure in the affection
Of your loved ones and your friends.

Bickleigh in Devon –
a charming corner of England

Elegant blooms of the common toadflax or linaria vulgaris

GOD'S MEDICINE

My medicine shall be the flowers
That blossom wild and free
My tonic shall be friendly letters
Sent with love to me.

My light shall be the glimpse of Heaven
Shining bright and blue
As if the clouds had parted
Just to let God's goodness through.

Cranborne Chase, Dorset is a popular place for a country walk

DAYBREAK

In the early hours of the morning
When the dawn is breaking through
There comes a lull in life
Before the day beings anew.

And then the birds start singing
Even louder with the light
As if their grateful voices
Plan to put the whole world right.

This is the hour to wake and wonder
Fit your heart with wings that soar
To buckle on your faith
And face whatever is in store.

At last – feeding time for these young linnets

Rolling countryside near Bath, Avon

Side by side in Aldeburgh, Suffolk

MY NURSE

Dear nurse, you are my confidante
My light, my corner stone.
The greatest personality
That I have ever known.

Your smile is bright and beautiful
Your work is never done
Yet to a dreary duty
You bring a sense of fun.

You tease me when I thank you
For I cannot write a letter
But from my heart I bless my nurse
Who helped to make me better.

Gold Hill in Shaftesbury, Dorset – unchanged over the centuries

RAINBOWS IN THE SKY

Why does the sun pierce the mists of the morning?
Why does a rainbow smile out of the rain?
Why does the silver line cling to the billows
And earth after storms have a joyful refrain?

Just as a proof that the dark days are passing
That shadows are made by the light of the sun.
That life may look black for the space of a season
But there is a rainbow for everyone.

Charming view of Snowshill, Gloucestershire

Snowdon's impressive peaks, as viewed from Talsarnau, Harlech

TO WISH YOU WELL

May you have sweet music
For the soothing of your mind
A good book for your leisure
And companions who are kind.

May you see wide vistas
Through a window that is small
And have the world brought to you
By the friends who come and call.

A host of daffodils adds the final touch
– Tissington, Derbyshire

Tranquil scene in the New Forest village of Swan Green

BORROWED JOY

Let's borrow from our memories
When times are sad and trying
Let's find a little laughter
When we're very near to crying.

Secure in loving thought
Of happy friends and distant places
Knowing future days will hold
Good times and merry faces.

This hay cart is a colourful reminder of bygone days

THINKING OF YOU

May you soon be walking
In the meadows cool and green
Breathing scent and sunshine
Where the landscape is serene.

May you soon be laughing
With your family and friends
Visiting and entertaining
When this ordeal ends.

Singing while you work
The way you do, and sharing fun
While giving joy to other folk
As you have always done.

Follow my leader, swan-style

St. Bridget's and St. Bega's Church by
Bassenthwaite Lake, Cumbria

Picturesque Lochan on the Forest Trail, Glencoe, Highland

DON'T WORRY

Let your worries be worthwhile
Don't lift a stone or hump a load
Nor climb a mountain or a stile
Before you meet it on the road.

Never spend a sleepless night
Before you feel the dreaded pain
Nor set upon the day a blight
For fear old woes occur again.

The serene waters of Loch Doon, Dumfries and Galloway

A CHILD'S PRAYER

Lord Who made the sunset
So that dusk was not forlorn
Who lined the clouds with silver
Hung the dewdrops on the dawn.

Lord Who shaped the petals
Of the daisy and the rose
Give Your courage to a child
When day is at a close.

Take this little prayer of mine
And give it shining wings
To find its way to heaven
Full of thanks for lovely things.

Daisies such as these are always a cheering sight

Splendid display of roses at Castle Howard, Yorkshire

I BELIEVE

Who can view the night and day
The sunset and the dawn
And yet deny Thy hand, Thy work
Or treat one leaf with scorn?

Though men have many talents
For inventions here below
Can man design one blade of grass
And make that blade to grow?

A spider's web, so frail a thing
Yet in the morning dew
Can shine forth like a diadem
And bear the weight of dew.

Who can trap a snowflake
Or grow a flower from seed
And doubt the Lord will not be near
To help us in our need?

Tredington, Cotswolds – a charming
village in the heart of England

Guernsey is a perfect place to get away from it all

HEALING HANDS

Put your life in God's good keeping
Let your cares be borne away
For healing hands are waiting
To make you strong today.

There are prayers for your well-being
There are wishes of good cheer
And kindly thoughts surrounding you
From people far and near.

May your thoughts be brave and beautiful
Your spirits high and strong
Then faith that blossoms in the heart
Will carry you along.

Colourful harbour at Lyme Regis, Dorset

STEADFAST

Be thankful for the loving heart
That always stays the same
The one who stands beside you
Sharing failure, fun or fame

Whose ways will never alter
Whose eyes will always smile
Even though you haven't been
So cheerful for a while.

One who loves you just as much
Though happy or depressed
In sickness or in health
When at your worst or at your best.

This red setter has his heart set on something . . . .

Man's other best friend?

MY DAY

Say to yourself as you go on your way
I am going to be better and better today
There's a purpose for living, a reason for fun
And I shall be friendly with everyone.

Say to yourself 'I refuse to frown'
There is nothing so bad it can pull me down
There are friendly faces and I shall see one
There are happy people and I shall be one.

At anchor in Seaton Harbour, River Axe

Standing the test of time is High Ham Mill, Somerset

A quiet corner at St. Michael's Church, Axmouth, Devon

SILENT PRAYERS

Receive my silence, Lord
When I am lost for words to pray
Look deep into my heart
And read the words I cannot say.

I long to tell my fears
But daren't, in case I fear anew.
In silence and humility
I bring my cares to You.

Hear me, help me, love me
Because You know I care.
And in my silence read
A feeble, but fervent prayer.

Quaint cottage in the lush English countryside

STEPPING STONES

They tumble over stepping stones
The waterfalls of life
In smooth or roaring torrents
Above the foam of strife.

Laughing with the sunbeams
And weeping with the rain
Into the quiet waters
Of a peaceful life again.

Rushing waters of aptly named Watersmeet, Lynmouth, Devon

Dramatic scenery in Dovedale, Derbyshire

Looking for a bargain – Bridport Market, Dorset

GOOD COMPANIONS

We miss your sense of humour
That comes from a happy heart.
We miss the joyous outings
In which you took your part.

Our sympathy is with you
And good wishes by the host.
Good friend and kind companion
'Get well quickly' is our toast.

The medieval charm of Elm Hill, Norwich attracts many visitors

Waves crash relentlessly at Land's End

FRIEND OF MINE

Fear not dear friend. Sleep well, be brave,
In peace of mind your strength to save
Lean on the one who understands
Trust in the skill of healing hands.

Then every hour of every day
Will help you farther on your way
To health and vigour, free from dread
To live the happy life ahead.

A moment of perfect calm at Loch Linnhe, near Fort William

THE GARDEN AT DUSK

In the cool of a garden when evening draws in
Serenity waits where the shadows begin.
In the fragrance of dusk and the murmur of clover
The cares that we carry pass peacefully over.

Flowers in the fullness shed blessings about
And the turmoil of living fades quietly out.
Hope glimmers through with the evening star
And anxieties shrink to the size that they are.

Colourful array of chrysanthemums

Thomas Hardy's picturesque cottage at
High Buckhampton, Dorset

Sun lights up the whitewashed walls of Tharston Mill, Norfolk

RED CROSS GARDENER

Picking up the fallen roses broken by the rain
Staking battered dahlias that they may bloom again
Renovating trellis where the honeysuckle rambles
Rescuing the gladioli beaten in the brambles.
Like a Red Cross unit when the storms of battle cease
Comforting the wounded and bringing back the peace

The dahlia is magnificent in full bloom

WATCH FOR THE DAWN

Watch for the dawn to lift your fighting power
Wait for the light to change the darkest hour
Suffering is borne by holding on and hoping
Daring to live by keeping on and coping.

You, even you, are braver than you know
And stronger than you think, when progress is slow
Watch for the dawn throughout the darkest night
And join the birds singing with the morning light.

Light and shade harmonise in this view
of Clovelly Beach, Devon

A gaze that melts the hardest heart

A WELCOME WAITS

You mean so much, so very much
To those who love you well
Even the pets are waiting
With a 'welcome home' to tell.

The home is drear without you
And the neighbours miss your smile
And friends are sending wishes
For your welfare all the while.

These kittens make an irresistable duo

JUST FOR YOU

Make a brave new start today
As if the world were new
As if the dawn were breaking
Especially for you.

As if the singing rivers
Were rippling through your heart
Lift your spirits, lift your eyes
And make a brave new start.

Loch Ranza, Arran — a perfect place to get away from it all

Spectacular Rogie Falls near Contin, Strathpeffer

GIFTS OF LOVE

A gift of love, a gift of flowers
Lends beauty to the passing hours.
Fond thoughts from those who are apart
Bring comfort to the weary heart.

A letter from a friend who cared
Recalls a memory once shared.
And all the wishes loved ones tell
Combine this day to make you well.

The common fuschia displays its exquisite blooms

Whether in sickness or in health, a flower arrangement
is always appreciated

The setting sun reflected in the River Bure, Acle, Norfolk

LOOKING OUTWARDS

Take your hand in mine for comfort
Put your trust in God for love
Looking out to the horizon
There's a shining light of love.

No person could be dearer
No wishes more sincere
All the blessings for your safety
Are surrounding you my dear.

On eternal watch – Dartmoor's Old Man of the Moors,
near Manaton

CHOOSING A GIFT

I wish I could send the midnight star
To shine with a healing light
Or the colours of dawn, when your heart is forlorn
In the lonely hours of the night.

The noonday hush, or the song of a thrush
To give you a moment of pleasure
Good wishes I'd thread, for pearls round your bed
If I could, to be read at your leisure.

Somerset's beautiful rolling landscape as viewed
from Haddon Hill

A beauty spot near the hamlet of Friday Street,
on the North Downs

Looking down to Netherdale Farm, Monsal Dale, Derbyshire

CROSSING THE BRIDGE

You'll be crossing the bridge to a life that is new
You'll be moving along with the stream
You'll be facing the world with a different view
And climbing the hill of your dream.

So you'll need all the courage that you can find
All the wishes that we can give
May the joy you have given come back to mind
To bless you as long as you live.

Spectacular scenery follows the River Earn, Comrie, Tayside

SOMEBODY CARES

There's never a singing river
Without solace in its song
And never a winding way
That travels uphill all along.

There's never a night so dreary
That dawn forgets to break
Nor time when someone does not smile
For someone else's sake.

Lindean, Borders provides the ideal location for a spot of fishing

Brightly coloured boats on the River Wey at Guildford

Horsey Mill — a popular stopping place for Broads holidaymakers

FORGET-ME-NOT

How could I forget you
This flower that speaks your name
Bonny, blue and beautiful
It always stays the same.

Dancing in a sweet warm world
Where views are tender green
Where days are fair and fragrant
And the twilight is serene.

Small and frail and lovable
How many hours you bless
I look for you to borrow peace
Then share your happiness.

It's always a pleasure to spot the forget-me-not's vivid blooms

REMEMBERING YOU

When I was sad I thought of you
And all the woe you had been through
Suffering more than your share
Too much for one lone soul to bear.

Yet I have never seen you cry
You always held your head so high
And faced the world and went your way
Although your heart wept with dismay.

Your courage was a star heaven sent
That showed me what true valour meant
Then when my own poor pluck seemed gone
I thought of you . . . and carried on.

Boats jostle for space at Torquay
harbour in Devon

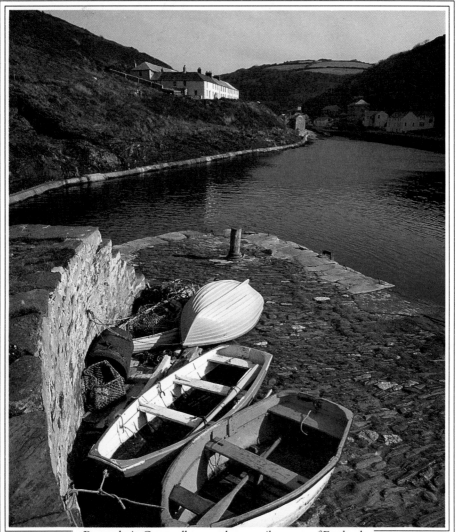
Boscastle, in Cornwall – a truly unspoilt corner of England

TURN OF THE TIDE

Brave heart, brave spirit, you will battle through
To good health and horizons that are new.
Look straight ahead and deal not with dismay
The light is there to guide you on your way.

Let faith be yours to face what is to be
The tide will turn upon the darkest sea
Brave heart, brave spirit with a gentle soul,
God hear our prayers, and hearing make you whole.

Dramatic rocky coastline at Godrevy Point, Cornwall

GOODNIGHT
AND GOD BLESS YOU

Peace and the purple twilight
Shadows of silent trees
Billows that fold, like the cloth of gold
Where none but an angel sees.

Peace and the evening murmurs
Of leaves being lulled to rest
And the fading glory of sunset's story
Which the love of the Lord hath blessed.

Evening skyline awash with nature's glorious hues

ISBN 0-7117-0348-5 © *Copyright Jarrold Colour Publications 1988. Designed and produced by Parke Sutton Limited, Norwich for Jarrold Colour Publications, Norwich. Origination by Blackfriars Colour Repro, Norwich. Printed in Portugal.*